D0690179

cx

Superfast TRUCKS

by Donna Latham

Consultant: Paul F. Johnston, Washington, D.C.

BEARPORT
PUBLISHING

New York, New York

Credits

Cover and Title Page, © Rusty Jarrett / Getty Images; 4, © George Tiedemann / NewSport / Corbis; 5, © Chris Stanford / Getty Images; 6, © Top Secret Communication + Design inc.; 7, © Top Secret Communication + Design inc.; 8–9 © Top Secret Communication + Design inc.; 10, © AP Photo / Bob Jordan; 11, © Royalty-Free / Corbis; 12, © Sam Sharpe / Corbis; 13, © Rusty Jarrett / Getty Images; 14, © Reuters / CORBIS; 15, © Robert Laberge / Getty Images; 16, © AP Photo / Glenn Smith; 17, © AP Photo / David Graham; 18, © AP Photo / Chris O'Meara; 19, © AP Photo / Glenn Smith; 20, © Top Secret Communication + Design inc.; 21T, © Streeter Lecka / Getty Images; 21B, © Jamie Squire / Getty Images; 22, © Top Secret Communication + Design inc.; 23, © AP Photo / Glenn Smith; 24T, © AP Photo / Orlin Wagner; 24B, © UPI Photo / Malcolm Hope / Newscom; 25, © AP Photo / Ron Sanders; 26, © Jonathan Ferrey / Getty Images; 27, © AP Photo / Chris O'Meara; 29, © Top Secret Communication + Design inc.

Publisher: Kenn Goin
Editorial Development: Judy Nayer
Creative Director: Spencer Brinker
Original Design: Paula Jo Smith

Library of Congress Cataloging-in-Publication Data

Latham, Donna.

  Superfast trucks / by Donna Latham.

      p. cm.–(Ultimate speed)

  Includes bibliographical references and index.

  ISBN-13: 978-1-59716-253-1 (library binding)

  ISBN-10: 1-59716-253-1 (library binding)

  ISBN-13: 978-1-59716-281-4 (pbk.)

  ISBN-10: 1-59716-281-7 (pbk.)

  1. Automobiles racing–Juvenile literature. 2. Trucks–Juvenile literature. 3. Truck racing–Florida–Daytona Beach–Juvenile literature. 4. Martin, Mark, 1959- I. Title. II. Series.

  TL230.15.L38 2006

  629.223'2–dc22

                              2006012512

For more information, write to Bearport Publishing Company, Inc., 101 Fifth Avenue, Suite 6R, New York, New York 10003. Printed in the United States of America.

10 9 8 7 6 5 4 3 2 1

CONTENTS

At the Speedway

Mark Martin was ready for his first big race of the year. He was already one of NASCAR's (National Association for Stock Car Auto Racing) top drivers. Yet on February 17, 2006, Martin was not racing a car. Instead, he was sitting behind the wheel of a truck. He was about to race in the GM FlexFuel 250 in Daytona Beach, Florida. It was the first full season that Martin was racing trucks.

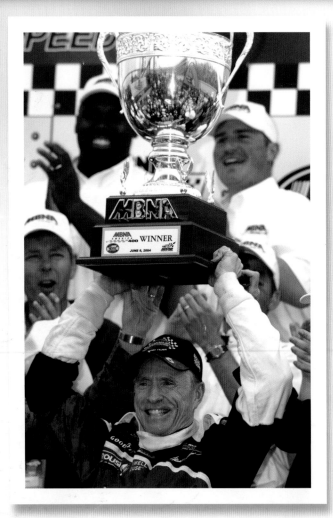

Before racing trucks, Martin had won many car races. Here, Martin celebrates winning the MBNA 400 on June 6, 2004.

"I hadn't planned on racing this race," Martin said. Another driver on Martin's team, David Ragan, turned over the truck to him the night before. "It wound up a last-minute surprise," said Martin.

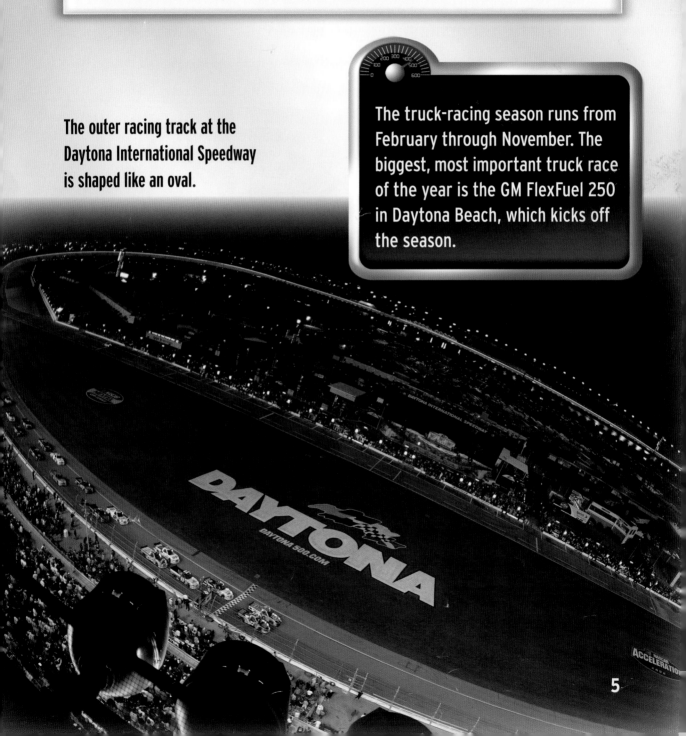

The outer racing track at the Daytona International Speedway is shaped like an oval.

The truck-racing season runs from February through November. The biggest, most important truck race of the year is the GM FlexFuel 250 in Daytona Beach, which kicks off the season.

On the Starting Grid

Martin had been handed the yellow and green #6 Ford just in time to race in the **qualifying laps**. He zoomed around the track in 50.384 seconds. Martin got the fastest qualifying time that day.

Martin's racing truck

Martin's average speed during his qualifying lap was 178.628 miles per hour (287.47 kph).

As the race was about to begin, Martin and his 35 **competitors** arranged themselves on the Daytona International Speedway's starting grid. The starting grid contains marked lines. At each line, a number shows exactly where a truck will begin the race. At the front of the track are the drivers with the fastest qualifying times. Martin had the best starting spot on the track—the inside front row.

Before the race begins, drivers take their positions on the starting grid.

NASCAR Craftsman Truck Series

Truck racing began as a branch of auto racing. In 1993, a team of racers built the first racing pickup trucks. To see how fans would react, the group introduced their trucks at a 1994 car-racing event—the Daytona 500. Throughout the season, pickups roared along racetracks in **exhibition races**.

Exhibition races are just for fun. They allow drivers to show off their skills to fans.

Like auto racing, truck racing thrills its fans.

Crowds roared, too. They loved the trucks. So in 1995, NASCAR created its first truck-racing series.

In 1996, with the backing of Craftsman Tools, the series became the NASCAR Craftsman Truck Series. Since then, truck racing has steadily picked up speed.

Beware of Dangers

NASCAR truck races cover shorter distances than auto races. They are usually 150 to 250 miles (241 to 402 km) long. Most car races are 500 to 600 miles (805 to 966 km) long. The Daytona 250 that Martin raced in covered 250 miles (402 km).

Flying pieces of trucks may shower the track during a wreck.

Both truck and auto racing are very dangerous. A truck can skid off the track in a **spinout**. It can even crash. When a wreck occurs, **officials** fly a yellow caution, or warning, flag. The flag tells drivers to beware of dangers on the track. Martin hoped he could make the 100 laps around the 2.5-mile (4-km) track in Daytona without crashing.

A yellow caution flag

Officials fly yellow caution flags if wrecks, darkness, or poor weather threaten the race.

Protecting the Drivers

Martin and the other racers faced dangers at every turn. At **breakneck** speeds, truck racing can cause serious injuries and even death. The threat of crashes is constant.

To stay safe, racers are strapped into seats connected to roll cages. A roll cage is a frame made of heavy steel tubes. It helps stop the truck's hard metal body from crushing the driver during a crash.

This driver is safely strapped into his seat and ready to race.

The racers also wear full-face helmets that guard their heads. The helmets protect drivers from breaking bones in their faces if their heads slam into their steering wheels. In case of explosions, racers wear **fire-retardant** suits and gloves.

The pit crew in action

A team of workers called the **pit crew** is ready to refuel and repair trucks during the race. Members of the team wear helmets and fire-retardant clothing.

A Fiery Wreck

The risk of crashes casts a shadow over the races. In 2000, Geoffrey Bodine experienced a horrifying wreck. During the Daytona 250, Bodine's truck slammed into a wall and exploded into flames. Flipping end over end, it became a fireball. Other trucks smashed into it.

At 190 miles per hour (306 kph), Bodine's truck smashed into the wall and became a rolling fireball.

The wreck took out 13 trucks and ripped off part of the safety fence. It threw **debris** into the crowd, injuring nine fans. People were certain Bodine was dead. He had serious injuries, but amazingly, he lived.

"I survived one of the worst crashes in the history of NASCAR," Bodine said.

Geoffrey Bodine's roll cage was almost all that remained from his truck's fiery wreck in 2000.

"Drivers, Start Your Engines!"

On the evening of February 17, 2006, Mark Martin geared up to race. A voice over a loudspeaker said to the excited crowd, "Are we ready to run the GM FlexFuel 250? Drivers, start your engines!" With a growl, engines fired.

Fireworks exploding over the track before the race

A **pace truck** with flashing yellow lights led the racers along the track so that they could get up to speed. After they completed three **pace laps**, the green flag was waved. As the pace truck turned off on Pit Road, drivers hit the gas. The race was on.

At Pit Road, trucks stop for refueling and repairs.

The green flag is waved and the race begins.

A Man with a Plan

At ultimate speeds, races change every instant. Most races are up for grabs until the final lap.

In 2005, driver Bobby Hamilton had been patient. He had **lagged** far behind the **pack**. By avoiding wrecks that took out other trucks, however, he had sped to victory in the last lap.

Bobby Hamilton after winning the 2005 Daytona 250

In 2006, several drivers were going to try the same thing—but not Martin. He had his own plan. He was going to try and stay in front for the whole race.

"If I wreck," he said, "I'll wreck in the front. If I get shuffled back, I'm going to do everything I can to get toward the front."

In the 2006 Daytona 250, 36 drivers began the race. Only 27 racers finished, however, because of wrecks and engine trouble.

The Leader of the Pack

True to his word, Martin immediately **seized** the lead. The energy was electric as he led a thick pack, three trucks wide. Not far behind, a second pack zipped along the straight section of the track. A third, smaller pack, was clustered behind them. These drivers might have been using Hamilton's **strategy**—playing it safe by staying in the back until the end.

Mark Martin leading the race ahead of Bill Lester (#22) and Mike Skinner (#5)

At lap four, Mike Skinner snatched the lead from Martin. Behind Skinner, a second driver, Bill Lester, zoomed past Martin, too. Now in single file, the front pack thundered forward.

"These cats have made some solid decisions," the announcer said.

Mike Skinner

Bill Lester

The straight section of an oval racetrack is called a straightaway. It has no bends or turns.

"Crazy Loose"

The trucks buzzed like a swarm of angry bees. With engines overheating at 275°F (135°C), drivers had to make unplanned pit stops. The torn-off windshield from one truck was stuck on top of another. The truck raced to the pit so the crew could rip it off.

Trucks take a beating at superfast speeds. Their bodies and tires may become loose. When this happens, it's hard for drivers to stay in control of their trucks.

One driver roared out of the pit with a wrench still hanging on his truck. He received a **penalty**.

The stress of the furious speed took its toll. Trucks wobbled. Drivers struggled for control.

"My truck is loose," Martin radioed the pit crew. "It needs to tighten up." He dropped behind.

"These trucks are crazy loose!" cried the announcer.

During a pit stop, Martin's crew changes tires and adds fuel.

Three Wild Wrecks

During lap 26, Joey Miller lost control of his truck. At 185 miles per hour (298 kph), it slid into the wall. The caution flag was flown, and Miller left the track for speedy repairs on his truck.

Joey Miller

Miller's truck slides out of control.

At lap 42, Mike Bliss, spinning like a Tilt-A-Whirl, crashed into Bill Lester. Four trucks tangled and bounced off walls.

For a time, a thick pack sped along the track. The trucks were tightly bunched together. Then, at lap 73, a third wreck took out seven trucks. Martin safely avoided each crash.

At top speeds, trucks can skid and crash into one another.

To allow the race to continue quickly after an accident, workers use the air from jet driers to blast debris off the track.

In the Blink of an Eye

On lap 81, Martin blasted to the front. He passed trucks as if they were standing still. Then, in the blink of an eye, he shuffled back to ninth position.

At lap 98, a spinout sent the fourth caution flag flying. It was time to battle out the final laps. Weaving between trucks, Martin grabbed the lead. Two drivers closed in on him.

Mark Martin waves the checkered victory flag.

26

Suddenly, at 170 miles per hour (273.6 kph), several trucks barreled off the track. Martin completed his final laps and won!

Motoring down Victory Lane, Martin waved the winner's flag. He said that he had loved the series before, "but I love it more now."

Confetti showers down on Martin and his truck in Victory Lane.

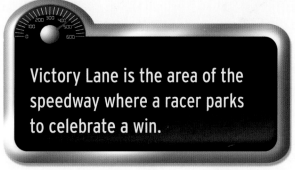

Victory Lane is the area of the speedway where a racer parks to celebrate a win.

JUST THE FACTS More About Truck Racing

- The GM FlexFuel 250 of 2006 lasted 1 hour, 44 minutes, and 21 seconds.

- The average speed of the racing trucks was 146.622 miles per hour (236 kph).

- The Daytona International Speedway has seats for 168,000 fans.

- According to NASCAR rules, drivers in the truck series must be at least 18 years old.

TIMELINE

This timeline shows the approximate times of Mark Martin's race to victory.

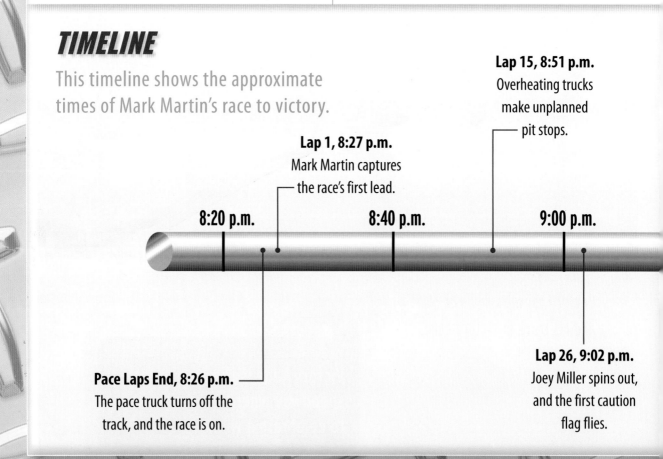

Lap 15, 8:51 p.m. Overheating trucks make unplanned pit stops.

Lap 1, 8:27 p.m. Mark Martin captures the race's first lead.

8:20 p.m.   8:40 p.m.   9:00 p.m.

Lap 26, 9:02 p.m. Joey Miller spins out, and the first caution flag flies.

Pace Laps End, 8:26 p.m. The pace truck turns off the track, and the race is on.

- Driver Kelly "Girl" Sutton has raced in more NASCAR Craftsman Truck Series than any other female. She is also the only racer known to have multiple sclerosis, a disease that has no cure.

Kelly "Girl" Sutton

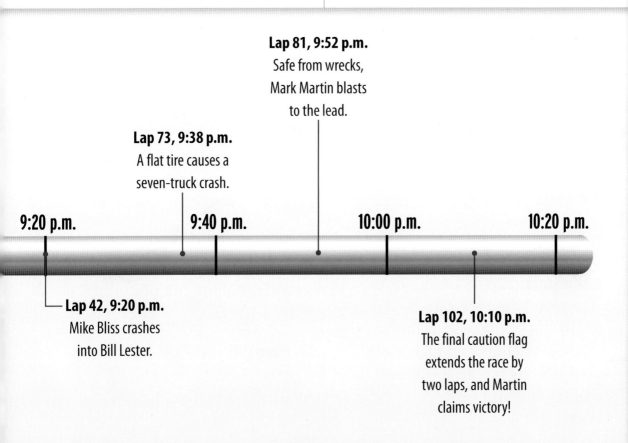

Lap 81, 9:52 p.m.
Safe from wrecks,
Mark Martin blasts
to the lead.

Lap 73, 9:38 p.m.
A flat tire causes a
seven-truck crash.

9:20 p.m. 9:40 p.m. 10:00 p.m. 10:20 p.m.

Lap 42, 9:20 p.m.
Mike Bliss crashes
into Bill Lester.

Lap 102, 10:10 p.m.
The final caution flag
extends the race by
two laps, and Martin
claims victory!

GLOSSARY

breakneck (BRAYK-nek) extremely fast to the point of being dangerous

competitors (kuhm-PET-uh-turz) people engaged in a contest, sport, or other competition

debris (duh-BREE) scattered pieces of something that has been wrecked or destroyed

exhibition races (*ek*-suh-BISH-uhn RAYSS-uhz) races held just for entertainment and to display drivers' skills

fire-retardant (FIRE-ri-TAR-dent) something that will not easily catch fire

lagged (LAGD) stayed behind

officials (uh-FISH-uhlz) people who enforce the rules during a race

pace laps (PAYSS LAPS) laps around the racetrack that all trucks make to warm up their engines and take their positions before the actual race begins

pace truck (PAYSS TRUHK) a truck that leads the racers during the pace laps and then leaves the track

pack (PAK) group

penalty (PEN-uhl-tee) a punishment for not following the rules

pit crew (PIT KROO) the workers in the pit area who take care of and fix the trucks during a race

qualifying laps (KWAHL-uh-*fye*-ing LAPS) the laps run before a race to find out which racers are fast enough to participate and what the starting order will be

seized (SEEZD) snatched; grabbed hold of

spinout (SPIN-out) the skidding and spinning out of control by a truck

strategy (STRAT-uh-jee) a plan

BIBLIOGRAPHY

Associated Press. "Bodine, Fans Injured in 13-Truck Accident." February 22, 2000.

Bechtel, Mark, and Mark Mravic. "Wheel to Live," *Sports Illustrated*. May 15, 2000.

Krall, Charles, ed. "Martin Flexes Muscle to Pick Up Daytona Glory," February 17, 2006. **www.truckseries.com/cgi-script/NCTS_06/articles/000062/006276-p.htm**

Krall, Charles, ed. *TrackSideLive!* GM FlexFuel 250, Daytona International Speedway, February 15–17, 2006. **www.truckseries.com/2006/TSLArchive/06r01-Daytona/index.htm**

Sports Network, The. "Martin Wins GM FlexFuel 250." February 17, 2006. **www.sportsnetwork.com/default.asp?c=sportsnetwork&page=nascar-t/news/ATN4005250.htm**

READ MORE

Bledsoe, Glen, and Karen E. Bledsoe. *The World's Fastest Trucks (Built for Speed)*. Mankato, MN: Edge Books (2002).

Graham, Ian. *Super Trucks (Fast Forward)*. Danbury, CT: Franklin Watts (2001).

Savage, Jeff. *The World's Fastest Pro Stock Trucks (Built for Speed)*. Mankato, MN: Capstone (2003).

Sessler, Peter, and Nilda Sessler. *Stock Trucks*. Vero Beach, FL: Rourke (1999).

LEARN MORE ONLINE

Visit these Web sites to learn more about truck racing:

www.nascar.com/races/truck/2006/1/index.html

www.nascar.com/series/truck/

www.truckseries.com/

INDEX

ABOUT THE AUTHOR

Donna Latham is a writer living near Chicago, Illinois. When Donna and her four brothers were kids, they set up looping toy racetracks in their basement and raced miniature trucks and cars.